Five Senses
Phonics

BOOK
3

Hunter Calder

A
FIVE SENSES
PUBLICATION

Five Senses Education Pty Ltd
2/195 Prospect Highway
Seven Hills NSW 2147 Australia
Phone   02 838 9265
Email   sevenhills@fivesenseseducation.com.au
Web   www.fivesenseseducation.com.au

Calder, Hunter
Five Senses Phonics Book 3
978-1-76032-424-7

Contents

About the Author

Multiple award-winning author Hunter Calder has extensive experience as a reading teacher, consultant, teacher trainer and lecturer, both in Australia and overseas. He obtained a Master of Arts from the University of Sydney and a Master of Education from the University of New South Wales. His many publications include the acclaimed *Reading Freedom 2000* series and the *Excel Basic English* books. He also contributed to the *Literacy Planet* online program.

The *Five Senses Phonics* series of early literacy skills is his most recent series of phonics books and is the outcome of collaboration with the experienced people at Five Senses Education.

Introduction

Welcome to *Five Senses Phonics*, a carefully structured series of activity books for pre-readers and beginning readers at the important stage of their literacy acquisition. The Five Senses activity books are intended for use in a preschool setting, in the beginning school years, and for older students who are having difficulty learning to read.

Book 3 continues the development of essential reading skills — basic phonics. The term 'phonics' refers a student's ability to hear and work with sounds in spoken words to reading them on the page. At this stage students work with sequences of individual sounds and form them into words. They learn, for instance, that the sounds 'b' - 'a' - 't' blend together to form the word 'bat'. Contemporary research tells us that students with good phonics skills go on to become competent readers. On the other hand, preschool age children and students in the early years at school who do not understand the relationship between spoken and written words are likely to develop literacy problems. Students who experience difficulty learning the skills of phonics may need the services of a specialised teacher trained in the development of auditory perception techniques.

The exercises are structured to allow the student to attain competence with the skills of phonics to develop their reading ability. On completing Book 3, students are able to read words containing single letter-sound relationships. Students then progress to Book 4 to work with words containing initial and terminal blends ('st' as is 'stop', 'cl' as in 'clap', 'nd' as in 'hand' and so on).

Student progress should regularly be monitored and evaluated after completing each level, using the Achievement Tests section which is specifically designed for teachers to assess effectiveness and so students can see the positive results of their learning experiences.

Instructions for Book 3

Sound Charts

Single Letter-Sound Correspondences: Vowels

Say the sounds for these letters.

a   as   in

e   as   in

i   as   in

o   as   in

u   as   in

1

Sound Charts

Single Letter-Sound Correspondences: Consonants

Say the sounds for these letters.

b   as   in

c   as   in

d   as   in

f   as   in

g   as   in

Sound Charts

Single Letter-Sound Correspondences: Consonants

Say the sounds for these letters.

h   as   in

j   as   in

k   as   in

l   as   in

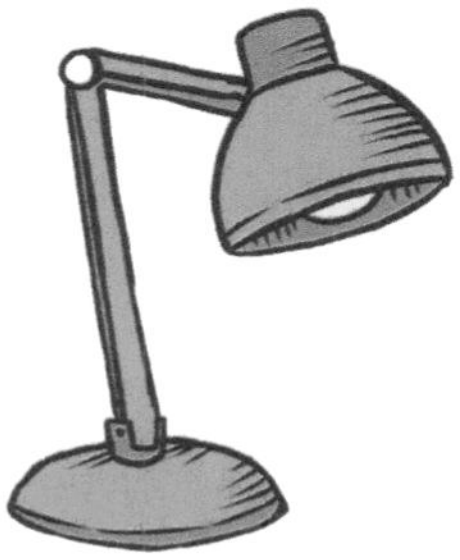

m   as   in

Sound Charts

Single Letter-Sound Correspondences: Consonants

Say the sounds for these letters.

n   as   in

p   as   in

r   as   in

s   as   in

t   as   in

Sound Charts

Single Letter-Sound Correspondences: Consonants

Say the sounds for these letters.

V   as   in

W   as   in

X   as   in

y   as   in

z   as   in

5

Sight Vocabulary

Learn these lists of sight words

a	in	and	saw	into	this
am	is	are	she	play	what
as	it	for	the	said	when
by	Mr	her	too	then	will
he	no	him	was	they	with
if	of	Mrs	why		
	on	not	yes		
		out	you		

Basic Sight Vocabulary

Can I read these words?

List One		List Two	
and	look	at	man
are	my	away	me
boy	of	big	not
can	play	blue	on
come	red	down	one
funny	run	for	ran
go	said	good	saw
he	says	green	three
is	see	have	too
jump	the	here	up
like	this	in	watch
little	to	it	you

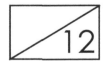 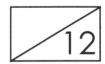 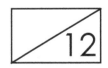 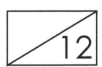

Yes I can!

Basic Sight Vocabulary

Can I read these words?

List Three		**List Four**	
all	going	an	had
am	home	after	help
around	into	as	her
black	make	be	him
but	no	brown	his
by	old	cold	if
call	out	did	she
came	was	ever	some
do	we	fly	stop
eat	will	from	two
fast	yellow	girl	who
get	yes	give	woman

 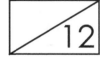 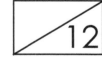

Yes I can!

Basic Sight Vocabulary

Can I read these words?

List Five		List Six	
above	new	about	how
find	now	again	long
gave	over	always	or
got	put	any	them
has	round	ask	then
Its	school	ate	they
know	so	cannot	walk
let	soon	could	went
live	ten	does	were
made	that	father	what
many	under	first	when
may	your	found	with

☐/12   ☐/12   ☐/12   ☐/12

Yes I can!

Basic Sight Vocabulary

Can I read these words?

List Seven		List Eight	
because	once	brother	pull
Been	open	buy	show
Before	our	draw	sit
bring	say	drink	small
children	take	even	their
done	tell	fall	these
every	there	grow	think
goes	upon	hold	those
mother	us	hot	very
much	want	just	where
must	wish	keep	which
never	would	only	work

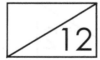 /12   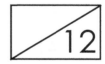 /12   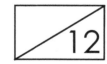 /12   /12

Yes I can!

10

Basic Sight Vocabulary

Can I read these words?

List Nine		List Ten	
best	pick	baby	Sing
better	please	daughter	sister
both	pretty	far	sleep
clean	read	house	something
cut	shall	hurt	son
eight	six	kind	start
five	today	laugh	thank
four	try	Mr	together
full	use	Mrs	warm
light	well	Own	wash
myself	why	right	water
off	write	seven	white

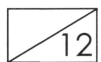 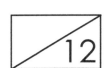 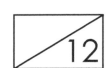 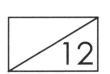

Yes I can!

11

Colour in the picture. Draw or paste other pictures with the 'a' sound on the page.

and   are   boy   can

Unit 1:2   Single Letter-Sound Correspondences: Short Vowel 'a' – 2

Write the letter for the missing vowel sound.

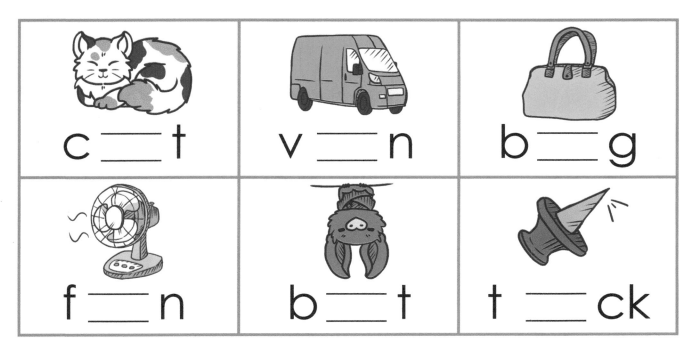

c __ t   v __ n   b __ g

f __ n   b __ t   t __ ck

Underline the word that matches the picture

1.   can   tap   bad   am

2.   dam   cab   pan   dad

3.   hat   man   mad   ham

4.   sad   jam   jab   fan

5.   ram   cat   van   pad

come   funny   go   he   (13)

Unit 1:3   Single Letter-Sound Correspondences: short vowel 'a' – 3

Say the rhyming words then write the missing word.

Draw a line to match the words that rhyme.

back	jab	ram	tap
gap	pack	wag	ham
nab	wax	pat	tag
tax	map	nap	mat

is   jump   like   little

Unit 1:4

Single Letter-Sound Correspondences: short vowel 'a' – 4

Circle the correct letters and then write the word.

	b c e a g d	_____
	f c a i h t	_____
	k f o a n l	_____
	h p u a t r	_____
	s t a e v p	_____

look   my   of   play   (15)

Unit 1:5   **Single Letter-Sound Correspondences: short vowel 'a' – 5**

Underline the word for each picture.

hat hats	pan pans
cap caps	bag bags

List the words with the same word pattern under each picture.

man	sat	nap	pat	gap
tan	map	rat	can	

_____   _____   _____

---------------------   ---------------------   ---------------------

_____   _____   _____

---------------------   ---------------------   ---------------------

_____   _____   _____

---------------------   ---------------------   ---------------------

(16)   **red   run   said   says**

Unit 1:6   Single Letter-Sound Correspondences: short vowel 'a' – 6

Draw a line from the picture to the matching word.

can
man
van

nap
tap
map

tack
sack
back

sat
fat
bat

Write the word that fits in the word shape box.

ran	sad	gap
tax	jam	dad
sat	wax	ram
dad	pack	wag

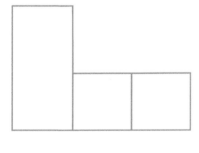
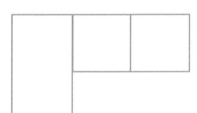
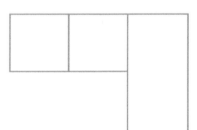

see   the   this   to   17

Unit 1:7   Single Letter-Sound Correspondences: short vowel 'a' – 7

Write the words for the pictures.

1. _____

2. _____

3. _____

4. _____

5. _____

6. _____

7. _____

8. _____

9. _____

18   at   away   big   blue

Unit 1:8   Single Letter-Sound Correspondences: short vowel 'a' – 8

Write the words for the pictures in the spaces shown by arrows.

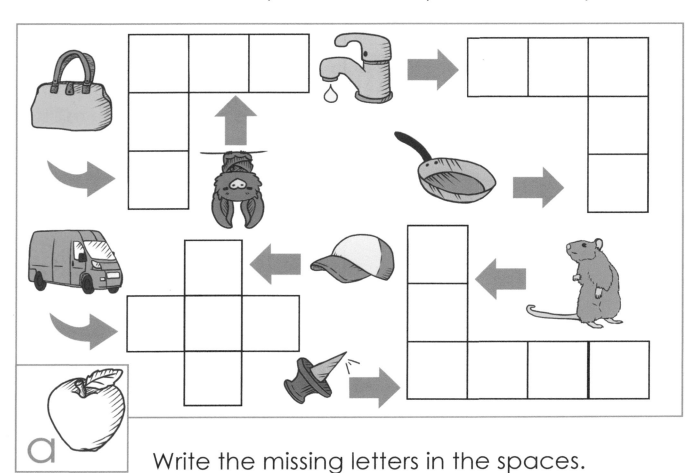

Write the missing letters in the spaces.

1. J.......ck h.........d .... b ....t.

2. The c..........t saw the f...............t r..........t.

3. P.........m s..........t in the v...........n.

4. J..........n h........d .... p.........ck on her b ....ck.

5. M.........tt r.........n with his d..........d.

down   for   good   green   (19)

Unit 1:9

Single Letter-Sound Correspondences: short vowel 'a' – 9

Tick the sentence that describes the picture.

☐ A rat in a sack.

☐ A rat in a rack.

☐ A man in a fan.

☐ A man in a pan.

☐ Sam and his ham.

☐ Sam and his jam.

☐ A bat and a cap.

☐ A bat and a map.

☐ A cat on a tack.

☐ A cat in a pack.

☐ Pam on the mat.

☐ Pam in her hat.

20   have   here   in   it

Write the word for the picture.

Write the word for the picture

1. The had a nap

2. Sam had a cap and a .

3. The ran up the rack.

4. Matt had ham in a  .

5. The sad man sat on a .

man   me   not   on   21

Unit 1:11   Single Letter-Sound Correspondences: short vowel 'a' – 11

Read the words as quickly and accurately as possible.

Can I read these words?

bad	bag	am	can
dad	rag	dam	fan
mad	sag	ham	man
pad	tag	jam	pan
sad	wag	ram	van
cap	bat	back	cab
gap	cat	pack	jab
map	hat	rack	nab
nap	pat	sack	tax
tap	sat	tack	wax

Time     /40   Right

Yes I can!

Unit 2:1   Single Letter-Sound Correspondences: short vowel 'e' – 1

Colour in the picture. Draw or paste other pictures with the 'e' sound on the page.

Unit 2:2   Single Letter-Sound Correspondences: short vowel 'e' – 2

Write the letter for the missing vowel sound.

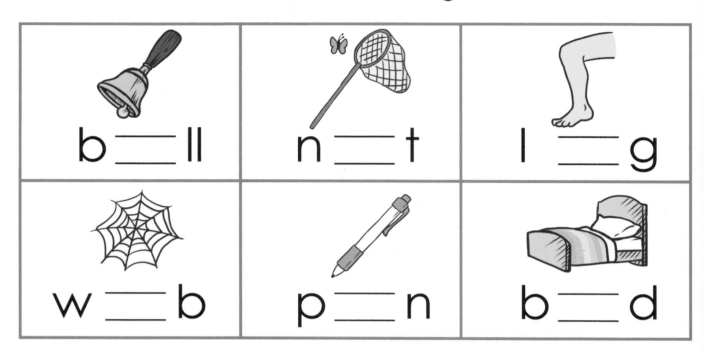

b __ ll   n __ t   l __ g

w __ b   p __ n   b __ d

Underline the word that matches the picture.

1.   sell   keg   hen   bet

2.   less   egg   yell   den

3.   beg   fell   men   jet

4.   ten   leg   bell   get

5.   mess   peck   well   let

(24)   too   up   watch   you

Unit 2:3   Single Letter-Sound Correspondences: short vowel 'e' – 3

Say the rhyming words then write the missing word.

hen _____

bell _____

net _____

men _____

Draw a line to match the words that rhyme.

den	led	beg	mess
fed	yell	less	leg
get	men	deck	bed
sell	let	red	neck

Unit 2:4   Single Letter-Sound Correspondences: short vowel 'e' – 4

Circle the correct letters and then write the word.

	z w	e a	c b	_____
	h y	i e	n x	_____
	b j	o e	c t	_____
	l d	e u	g f	_____
	h b	a e	k d	_____

(26)   but   by   call   came

Unit 2:5   Single Letter-Sound Correspondences: short vowel 'e' – 5

Underline the word for each picture.

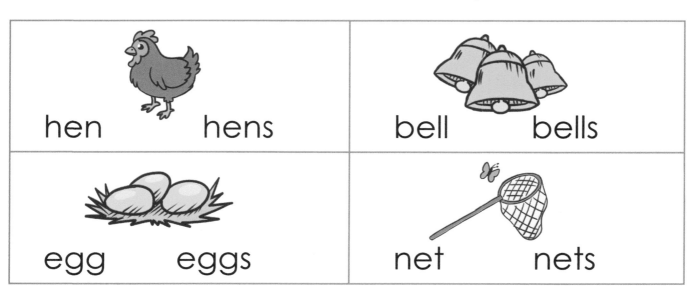

hen hens	bell bells
egg eggs	net nets

List the words with the same word pattern under each picture.

den   fed   sell   led   men

red   yell   fell   pen

do   eat   fast   get   (27)

Unit 2:6   Single Letter-Sound Correspondences: short vowel 'e' – 6

Draw a line from the picture to the matching word.

   led
bed
red

   leg
beg
map

   men
pen
hen

   get
jet
met

Write the word that fits in the word shape box.

web   less   neck

men   get   let

bed   egg   bell

mess   pen   den

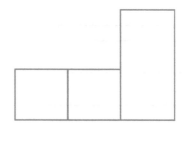   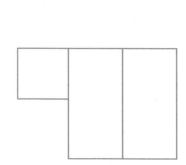   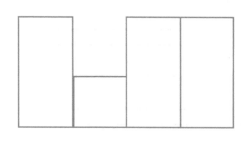

going   home   into   make

Unit 2:7

Single Letter-Sound Correspondences: short vowel 'e' – 7

Write the words for the pictures.

1 _____

2 _____

3 _____

4 _____

5 _____

6 _____

7 _____

8 _____

9 _____

no   old   out   was   (29)

Unit 2:8   Single Letter-Sound Correspondences: short vowel 'e' – 8

Write the words for the pictures in the spaces shown by arrows.

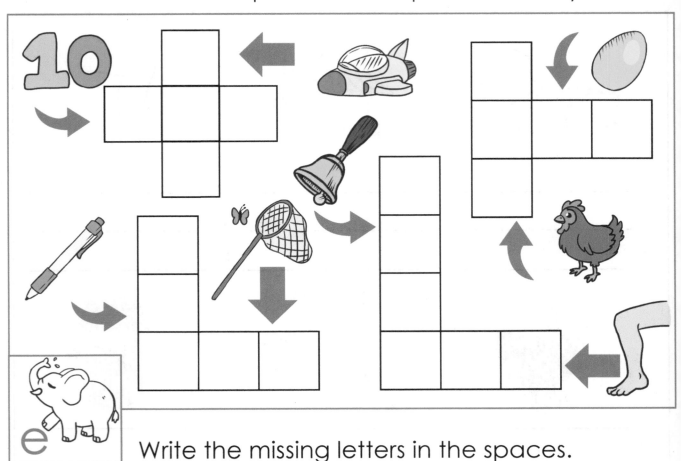

Write the missing letters in the spaces.

1. The r ....d h...........n was w ....t.

2. T...........d had t.............n p ....ns.

3. J...........n f...........ll out of b.........d.

4. The m........n l.........t T.........ss g.........t in the j........t.

5. R........x had an ....gg in his n...........t.

   we   will   yellow   yes

Unit 2:9

Single Letter-Sound Correspondences: short vowel 'e' – 9

Tick the sentence that describes the picture.

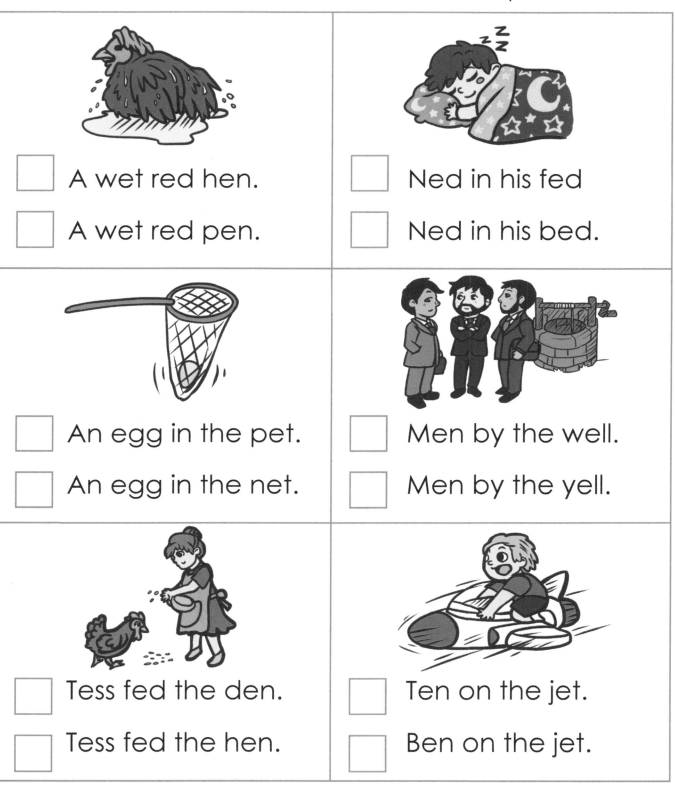

☐ A wet red hen.
☐ A wet red pen.

☐ Ned in his fed
☐ Ned in his bed.

☐ An egg in the pet.
☐ An egg in the net.

☐ Men by the well.
☐ Men by the yell.

☐ Tess fed the den.
☐ Tess fed the hen.

☐ Ten on the jet.
☐ Ben on the jet.

an   after   as   be   31

Write the word for the picture.

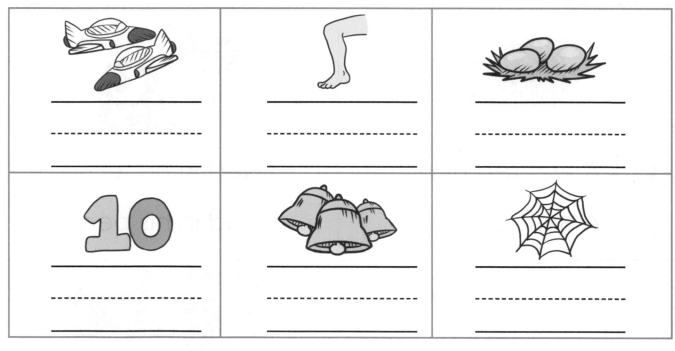

Write the word for the picture.

1. Rex fed the in the pen.

2. The was a mess.

3. The men let Ted go to the .

4. The web was by Meg's  .

5. Tess said, 'The  is in the den.

(32) brown   cold   did   ever

Unit 2:11   Single Letter-Sound Correspondences: short vowel 'e' – 11

Read the words as quickly and accurately as possible.

Can I read these words?

bed	den	bet	bell
fed	hen	get	fell
led	men	jet	sell
ned	pen	let	well
red	ten	net	yell

beg	less	deck	egg
keg	mess	neck	web
leg	tess	peck	yes

Time     /40   Right

Yes I can!

Unit 3:1   Single Letter-Sound Correspondences: short vowel 'i' – 1

Colour in the picture. Draw or paste other pictures with the 'i' sound on the page.

fly   from   girl   give

Write the letter for the missing vowel sound.

p __ n   b __ b   p __ g

p __ ll   l __ ps   k __ ck

Underline the word that matches the picture.

1   bid   dim   fit   zip

2   him   did   wig   sick

3   rim   six   lid   rig

4   fin   dig   bin   rid

5   big   hill   win   miss

had   help   her   him   35

Unit 3:3   Single Letter-Sound Correspondences: short vowel 'i' – 3

Say the rhyming words then write the missing word.

pin   _____   hill   _____

pig   _____   zips   _____

Draw a line to match the words that rhyme.

miss	fill	lick	sip
will	mix	nip	lid
pit	kiss	hid	dig
six	hit	rig	pick

    his   if   she   some

Unit 3:4

Single Letter-Sound Correspondences: short vowel 'i' – 4

Circle the correct letters and then write the word.

6	s l	i u	x m	_____
	n b	o i	p b	_____
	p r	i e	g f	_____
	t f	a i	n v	_____
	w p	i u	y n	_____

stop   two   who   woman   (37)

Unit 3:5   Single Letter-Sound Correspondences: short vowel 'i' – 5

Underline the word for each picture.

fin fins	pill pills
pin pins	bib bibs

List the words with the same word pattern under each picture.

rig   hip   pick   lip   sick

big   tick   dig   rip

above   find   gave   got

Unit 3:6   **Single Letter-Sound Correspondences: short vowel 'i' – 6**

Draw a line from the picture to the matching word.

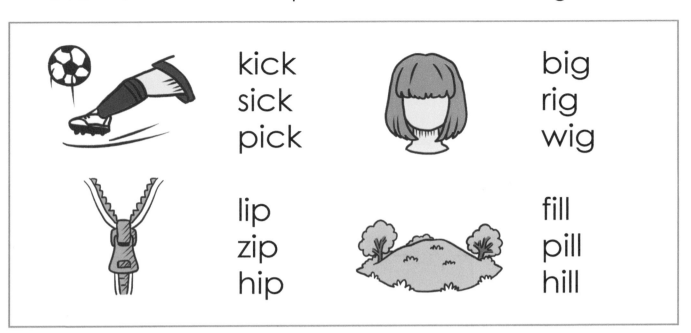

kick
sick
pick

big
rig
wig

lip
zip
hip

fill
pill
hill

Write the word that fits in the word shape box.

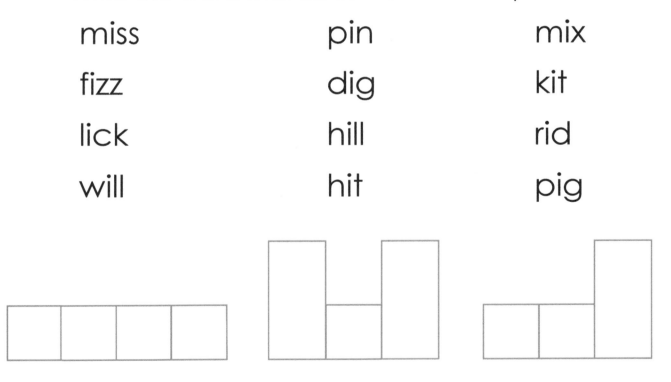

miss   pin   mix

fizz   dig   kit

lick   hill   rid

will   hit   pig

has   its   know   let   39

Unit 3:7   Single Letter-Sound Correspondences: short vowel 'i' – 7

Write the words for the pictures.

1. _____

2. _____

3. _____

4. _____

5. _____

6. _____

7. _____

8. _____

9. _____

40   live   made   many   may

Unit 3:8 Single Letter-Sound Correspondences: short vowel 'i' – 8

Write the words for the pictures in the spaces shown by arrows.

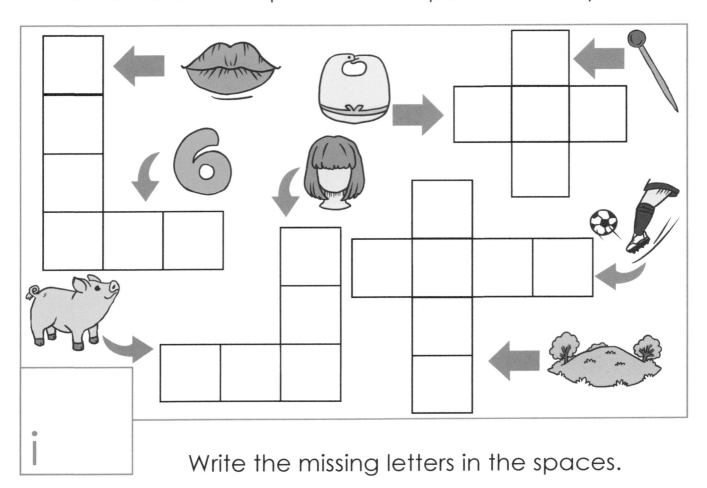

Write the missing letters in the spaces.

1. N.......ck b.......t h.......s l.......p.

2. D.........d S.......d k.......ss M....... ss F.......nn?

3. S.......x p....... ns are ....n the t....... n.

4. W.......ll T.......m m.......ss the k.......ck?

5. J.......ll h.......t the b.......n with her h.......p.

Unit 3:9

Single Letter-Sound Correspondences: short vowel 'i' – 9

Tick the sentence that describes the picture.

☐ A pig in a wig.

☐ A pig in a fig.

☐ Jill on the fill.

☐ Jill on the hill.

☐ A kid in a bib.

☐ A kid in a rib.

☐ Rick kicks the bin.

☐ Rick kicks the win.

☐ A zip in a dip?

☐ A zip in a lip?

☐ A lid on Kim.

☐ A rid on Kim.

42   round   school   so   soon

Write the word for the picture.

Write the word for the picture.

1. The had a big rip in it.

2. Will the fit Jill?

3. The  ran up the track.

4. Bill had **6** pins.

5. The will fit in the tin.

ten   that   under   your   43

Unit 3:11   Single Letter-Sound Correspondences: short vowel 'i' – 11

Read the words as quickly and accurately as possible.

Can I read these words?

bid	big	dim	bin	dip
did	dig	him	fin	hip
hid	pig	Jim	pin	lip
lid	rig	Kim	tin	nip
rid	wig	rim	win	zip

bit	fill	kick	hiss	fix
fit	hill	lick	kiss	mix
hit	Jill	pick	miss	six
kit	pill	sick	bib	fizz
pit	will	tick	rib	inn

Time ☐   ◻/50 Right

Yes I can!

Unit 4:1   Single Letter-Sound Correspondences: Short Vowel 'o' – 1

Colour in the picture. Draw or paste other pictures with the 'o' sound on the page.

about   again   always   any   45

Unit 4:2   Single Letter-Sound Correspondences: Short Vowel 'o' – 2

Write the letter for the missing vowel sound.

d __ ll	m __ p	r __ d
l __ ck	f __ x	p __ t

Underline the word that matches the picture.

1   cob   dog   cod   hop

2   pot   job   sock   pop

3   top   nod   mob   box

4   pod   hot   hop   rob

5   boss   rod   sob   off

(46)   ask   ate   cannot   could

Unit 4:3   Single Letter-Sound Correspondences: Short Vowel 'o' – 3

Say the rhyming words then write the missing word.

box   _____

rock   _____

top   _____

log   _____

Draw a line to match the words that rhyme.

job	nod	cot	rock
rod	top	box	got
fog	sob	loss	fox
pop	jog	dock	boss

does   father   first   found   47

Unit 4:4   Single Letter-Sound Correspondences: Short Vowel 'o' – 4

Circle the correct letters and then write the word.

	b c	o a	x d	_____
	f r	u o	d g	_____
	h d	o l	k g	_____
	t l	o e	p m	_____
	n f	a o	p x	_____

how   long   or   them

Unit 4:5   Single Letter-Sound Correspondences: Short Vowel 'o' – 5

Underline the word for each picture.

doll dolls	rod rods
pot pots	sock socks

List the words with the same word pattern under each picture.

fog   hop   pop   hog   dock

top   sock   jog   rock

then   they   walk   went   (49)

Unit 4:6   Single Letter-Sound Correspondences: Short Vowel 'o' – 6

Draw a line from the picture to the matching word.

mock
rock
dock

hop
lop
pop

not
rot
pot

rod
pod
nod

Write the word that fits in the word shape box.

cob   doll   nod

pod   loss   jog

moss   lock   off

hot   lot   fox

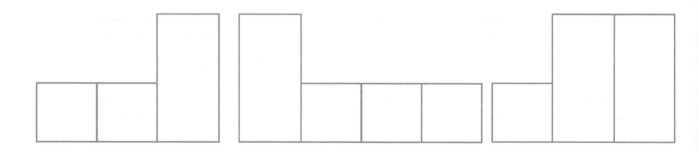

were   what   when   with

Unit 4:7   Single Letter-Sound Correspondences: Short Vowel 'o' – 7

Write the words for the pictures.

1._____   2._____   3._____

4._____   5._____   6._____

7._____   8._____   9._____

because   been   before   bring   (51)

Unit 4:8   Single Letter-Sound Correspondences: Short Vowel 'o' – 8

Write the words for the pictures in the spaces shown by arrows.

Write the missing letters in the spaces.

1. T........m g........t ....ff the d........ck.

2. The s........cks are n........t ....n the d........ll.

3. H........p ....n t........p of the l........g.

4. The d........g was h........t ....n the r........ck.

5. The b........ss had a l........ck ....n the b........x

children   done   every   goes

Tick the sentence that describes the picture.

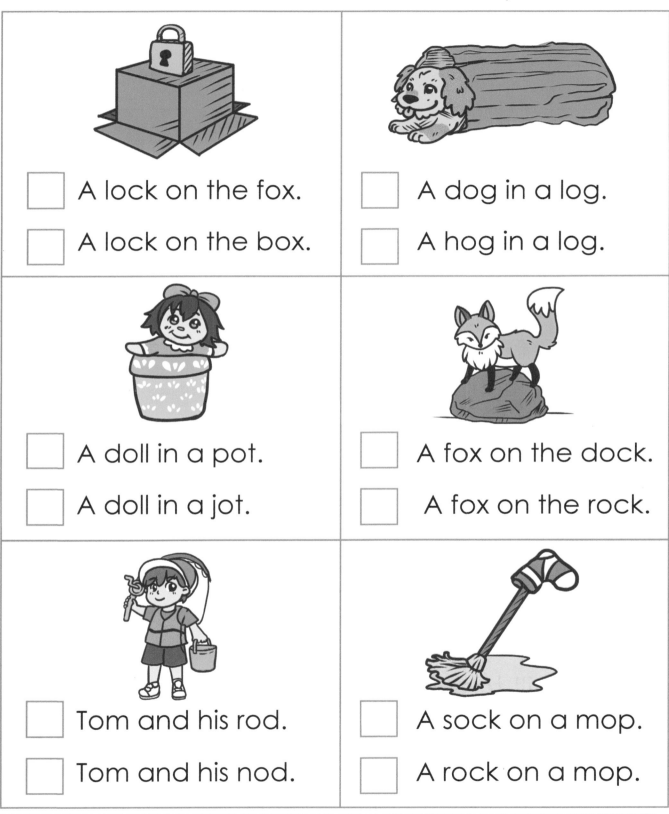

☐ A lock on the fox.
☐ A lock on the box.

☐ A dog in a log.
☐ A hog in a log.

☐ A doll in a pot.
☐ A doll in a jot.

☐ A fox on the dock.
☐ A fox on the rock.

☐ Tom and his rod.
☐ Tom and his nod.

☐ A sock on a mop.
☐ A rock on a mop.

mother   much   must   never   53

Write the word for the picture.

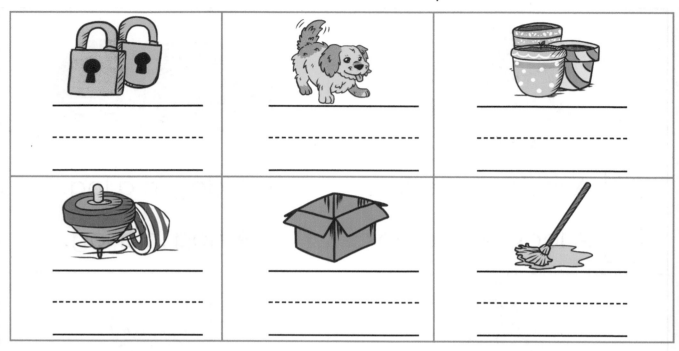

Write the word for the picture.

1. The hot dog got on the  . _____

2. Tom got a cod with his  . _____

3. Mrs Moss has lots of  . _____

4. Ron will toss the  . _____

5. The  sat on a box. _____

(54)   once   open   our   say

Read the words as quickly and accurately as possible.

Can I read these words?

cob	cod	dog	hop
job	God	fog	lop
mob	nod	hog	mop
rob	pod	jog	pop
sob	rod	log	top

cot	dock	ox	boss
got	lock	box	loss
hot	mock	fox	moss
lot	rock	off	doll
not	sock	on	Tom

Time [＿＿＿]   [／40] Right

Yes I can!

Unit 5:1   Single Letter-Sound Correspondences: Short Vowel 'u' – 1

Colour in the picture. Draw or paste other pictures with the 'u' sound on the page.

take   tell   there   upon

Unit 5:2   Single Letter-Sound Correspondences: Short Vowel 'u' – 2

Write the letter for the missing vowel sound.

| b __ s | d __ ck | r __ n |
| n __ t | t __ b | s __ n |

Underline the word that matches the picture.

1.   tug   cub   bus   fun

2.   hub   rug   but   cup

3.   gum   cut   run   rub

4.   luck   mug   tub   bun

5.   bug   dull   gun   hum

us   want   wish   would   57

Unit 5:3 Single Letter-Sound Correspondences: Short Vowel 'u' – 3

Say the rhyming words then write the missing word.

bug _____

gun _____

tug _____

pup _____

Draw a line to match the words that rhyme.

cub	gum	cup	tuck
hug	hut	luck	buzz
sum	rug	gull	pup
but	rub	fuzz	dull

brother   buy   draw   drink

Unit 5:4

Single Letter-Sound Correspondences: Short Vowel 'u' – 4

Circle the correct letters and then write the word.

	r s	u a	n t	_____
	c v	e u	p w	_____
	x n	i u	y t	_____
	b z	o u	s d	_____
	f b	u a	h g	_____

even   fall   grow   hold   59

Unit 5:5

Single Letter-Sound Correspondences: Short Vowel 'u' – 5

Underline the word for each picture.

duck ducks	cup cups
nut nuts	bug bugs

List the words with the same word pattern under each picture.

hug   cub   bun   fun   rug

hub   sun   rub   tug

hot   just   keep   only

Unit 5:6　　Single Letter-Sound Correspondences: Short Vowel 'u' – 6

Draw a line from the picture to the matching word.

　rug
hug
mug

　cut
nut
but

　cup
up
pup

　bun
fun
run

Write the word that fits in the word shape box.

fuss	hug	fun
bus	bud	gum
mutt	rub	cuff
tuck	cup	mud

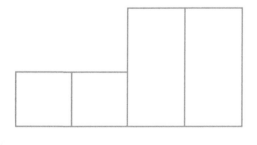
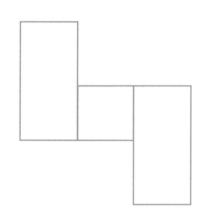
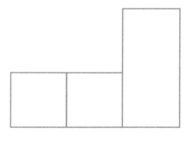

Unit 5:7   Single Letter-Sound Correspondences: Short Vowel 'u' – 7

Write the words for the pictures.

1. _____

2. _____

3. _____

4. _____

5. _____

6. _____

7. _____

8. _____

9. _____

62   their   these   think   those

Unit 5:8   Single Letter-Sound Correspondences: Short Vowel 'u' – 8

Write the words for the pictures in the spaces shown by arrows.

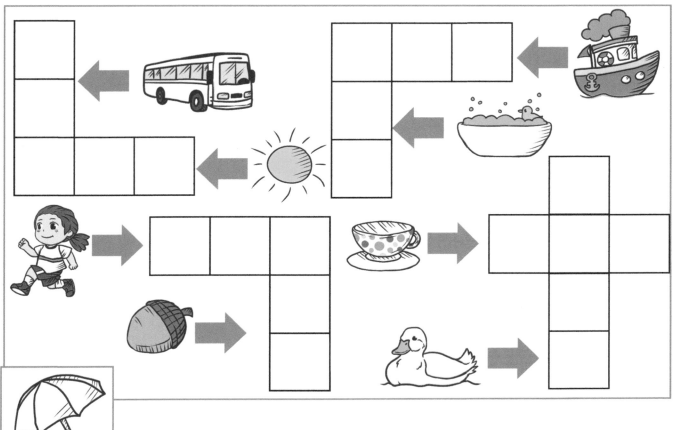

Write the missing letters in the spaces.

1. She is as sn........g as a b........g in a r........g.

2. M........m c........t the b........ns.

3. The p........p will r........n in the h........t.

4. G........s d........g in the m........d and the m........ck.

5. Do you h........ff and p........ff when you
   r........n and r........n?

Unit 5:9

Single Letter-Sound Correspondences: Short Vowel 'u' – 9

Tick the sentence that describes the picture.

☐ A buck on a rug.
☐ A duck on a rug.

☐ Run in the bun.
☐ Run in the sun.

☐ The pup is on us.
☐ The pup is on a bus.

☐ A cup on a nut.
☐ A cup in a hut.

☐ Russ in a rub.
☐ Russ in a tub.

☐ A bug on mum's cup.
☐ A hug on mum's cup.

(64)   best   better   both   clean

Unit 5:10 Single Letter-Sound Correspondences: Short Vowel 'u' – 10

Write the word for the picture.

Write the word for the picture.

1. The gulls are on the  .

2. The is in the tub.

3. Mrs Nunn has a ____ .

4. A ____ is in the hut.

5. I had to ____ to the bus.

Unit 5:11   Single Letter-Sound Correspondences: Short Vowel 'u' – 11

Read the words as quickly and accurately as possible.

Can I read these words?

cub	bug	gum	bun	but
hub	hug	hum	fun	cut
rub	mug	mum	gun	hut
tub	rug	rum	run	nut
sub	tug	sum	sun	rut

buck	dull	cuff	up	us
duck	gull	huff	cup	bus
luck	hull	muff	pup	fuss
muck	bud	ruff	buzz	muss
tuck	mud	mutt	fuzz	russ

Time [   ]   [/50] Right

Yes I can!

Unit 6:1   Single Letter-sound Correspondences: Short Vowels – 1

Colour in the pictures.

full   light   myself   off   67

Unit 6:2   Single Letter-sound Correspondences: Short Vowels – 2

Write the letter for the missing vowel sound.

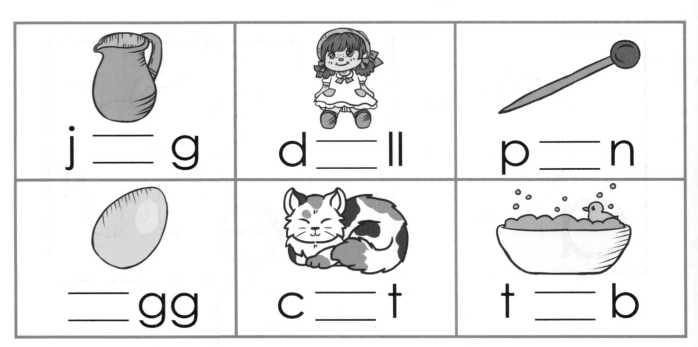

j __ g   d __ ll   p __ n

__ gg   c __ t   t __ b

Underline the word that matches the picture.

1.   mat   fox   men   lid

2.   hill   nod   fuss   tag

3.   tip   buzz   off   leg

4.   tuck   fan   mess   lick

5.   jam   dip   duck   hot

(68)   pick   please   pretty   read

Unit 6:3   Single Letter-sound Correspondences: Short Vowels – 3

Say the rhyming words then write the missing word.

pan _____

jet _____

wig _____

rock _____

Draw a line to match the words that rhyme.

dug	got	tax	bin
lot	deck	gull	wax
hit	rug	den	dull
neck	fit	fin	men

shall   six   today   try   69

Unit 6:4

Single Letter-sound Correspondences: Short Vowels – 4

Circle the correct letters and then write the word.

	h s o u n l	_____
	c m a u p n	_____
	r p a i n s	_____
	m t o e v p	_____
	w h e i x n	_____

use   well   why   write

Unit 6:5   Single Letter-sound Correspondences: Short Vowels – 5

Underline the word for each picture.

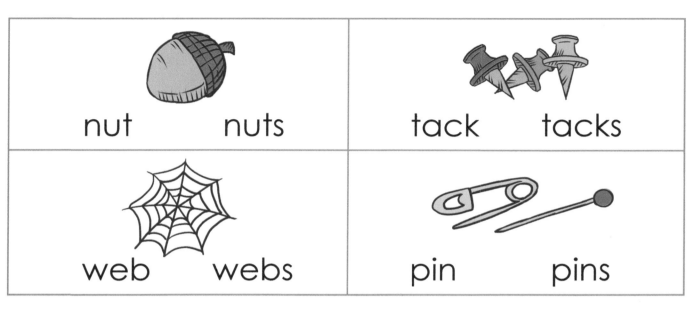

nut nuts	tack tacks
web webs	pin pins

List the words with the same word pattern under each picture.

fog   bun   log   fun   lap

run   tap   jog   nap

_____   _____   _____

baby   daughter   far   house   71

Unit 6:6   Single Letter-sound Correspondences: Short Vowels – 6

Draw a line from the picture to the matching word.

rub
tub
hub

jug
tug
bug

bag
sag
tag

bet
pet
net

Write the word that fits in the word shape box.

sock	neck	hid
nut	pack	yes
six	tell	log
mess	fuzz	get

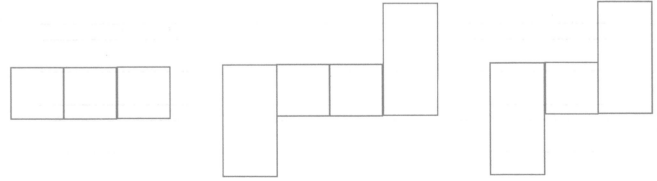

   hurt   kind   laugh   Mr

Write the words for the pictures.

1. _____

2. _____

3. _____

4. _____

5. _____

6. _____

7. _____

8. _____

9. _____

Mrs   own   right   seven   73

Unit 6:8   Single Letter-sound Correspondences: Short Vowels – 8

Write the words for the pictures in the spaces shown by arrows.

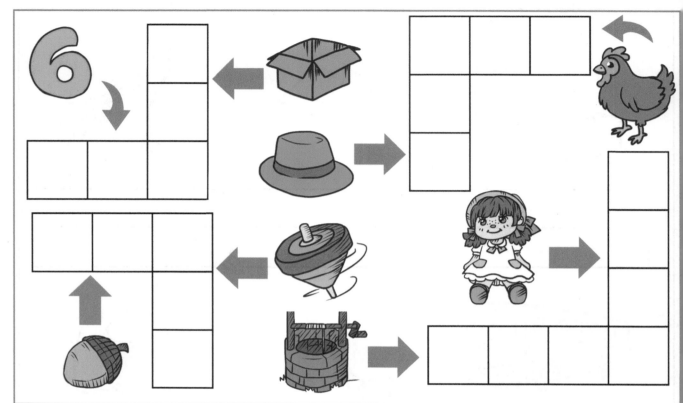

Write the missing letters in the spaces.

 1. The p......p d......g in the m......d.

 2. T......m and R......n had a j......g in the f......g

 3. J......ll was s......ck t......ll she had the p......lls

 4. T......ss l......d the h......n to the p......ns.

 5. D......d and J......ck s......t on the h......ts.

sing   sister   sleep   something

Tick the sentence that describes the picture.

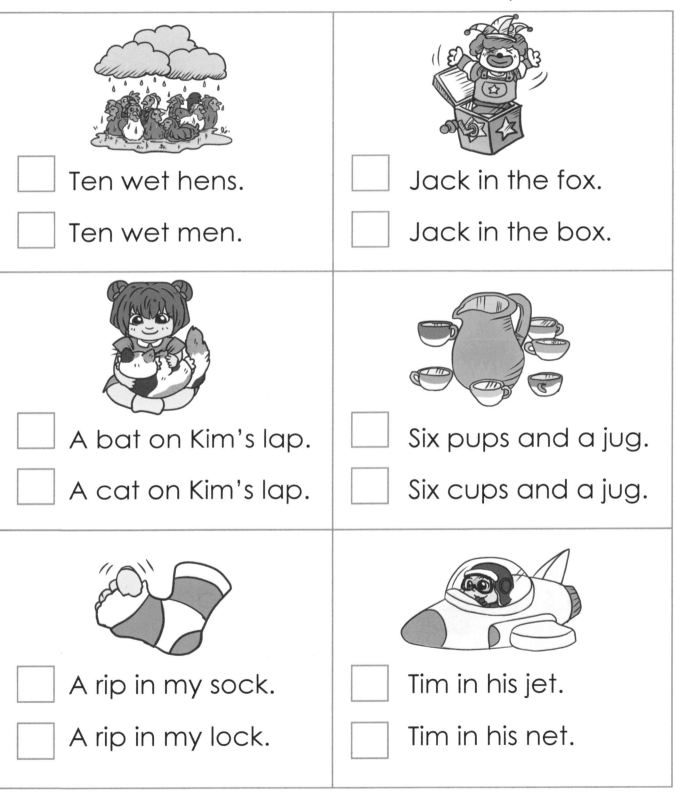

☐ Ten wet hens.

☐ Ten wet men.

☐ Jack in the fox.

☐ Jack in the box.

☐ A bat on Kim's lap.

☐ A cat on Kim's lap.

☐ Six pups and a jug.

☐ Six cups and a jug.

☐ A rip in my sock.

☐ A rip in my lock.

☐ Tim in his jet.

☐ Tim in his net.

son   start   thank   together   75

Write the word for the picture.

_____	_____	_____
- - - - - - - - - - -	- - - - - - - - - - -	- - - - - - - - - - -
_____	_____	_____
_____	_____	_____
- - - - - - - - - - -	- - - - - - - - - - -	- - - - - - - - - - -
_____	_____	_____

Write the word for the picture

1. Sam had **10** eggs and ham. _____

2. The hot dog ran at the  . _____

3. Dad's  fell off the dock. _____

4. Six socks are in the 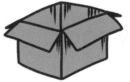 _____

5. Pat had a  on her lap. _____

(76) warm   wash   water   white

Read the words as quickly and accurately as possible.

Can I read these words?

can	men	hid	rob
cub	mad	red	big
nod	rug	rag	let
him	log	hum	ham
sell	win	hop	cut

mud	not	zip	beg
gap	luck	loss	fit
less	pat	dull	box
will	neck	jab	bus
lock	miss	yes	rack

Time     40 Right

Yes I can!

Achievement Tests

The Five Senses Phonics Achievement Tests complement each book in the Five Senses Phonics series. They are specifically designed to enable teachers to ensure that what has been taught remains current in the student's repertoire of skills. They can then identify areas that need reteaching or reinforcement.

The format of each Five Senses Phonics Achievement Test is identical to the equivalent book so students encounter activities with which they are familiar. Each test evaluates skills and sight words students have been taught. The careful design of the tests, ensures that the monitoring of progress is a positive and non-threatening exercise.

For ease of administration, the tests are photocopiable. The class record sheets and student record sheets allow the teacher to scan student performance on an individual or whole class basis. Taken as a group, the tests give a running record of each student's skill acquisition of the phonic hierarchy. Teachers who teach reading systematically and record student progress methodically will find the Five Senses Phonics First Achievement Tests an indispensable part of their teaching routine.

How to use these tests

The Five Senses Phonics Achievement Tests are intended to be an encouraging record of progress, not an intimidating assessment. The tests can be administered to individual students or the entire class. Allow approximately 30 minutes to complete each test.

Each group of tests contains one or two sight vocabulary tests. If administering the test to the class as a whole, have individual students read groups of sight words, then ask the class to read all sight words together. Keep watch for children who are having trouble, and test them later individually.

Maintain a positive attitude while administering the tests, and reward success with stickers, stamps and merit certificates. To attain mastery students should obtain at least 80 marks out of a possible 100. Any areas in the Test that indicate weakness should be retaught and then reinforced.

Test Record Sheet

Student .... Date...

Page	Test		
80	1	Word completion; word recognition	/11
81	2	Spelling; single letter-sound words	/12
82	3	Spelling; single letter-sound words	/5
85	4	Word recognition; word shape boxes	/7
86	5	Spelling; single letter-sound words	/ 9
87	6	Crossword puzzles; word completion.	/ 9
88	7	Sentence comprehension	/ 6
89	8	Singular-plural spelling; sentence completion	/11
90	9	Reading single letter-sound words	/ 30
		Knowledge of single letter-sound correspondence words	**Total** /100
91	10	**Basic sight vocabulary**	/40

Test 3:1

Word completion; word recognition

Write the letter for the missing vowel sound.

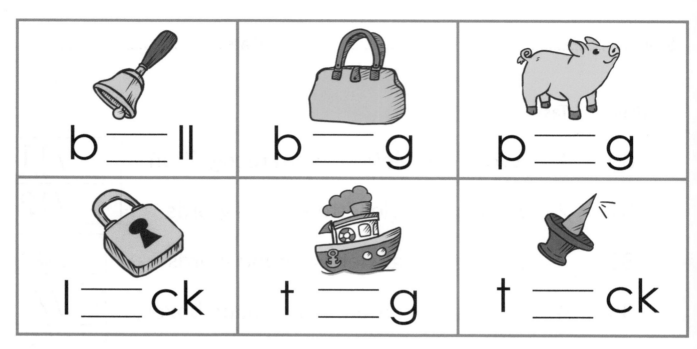

| b __ ll | b __ g | p __ g |
| l __ ck | t __ g | t __ ck |

Underline the word that matches the picture

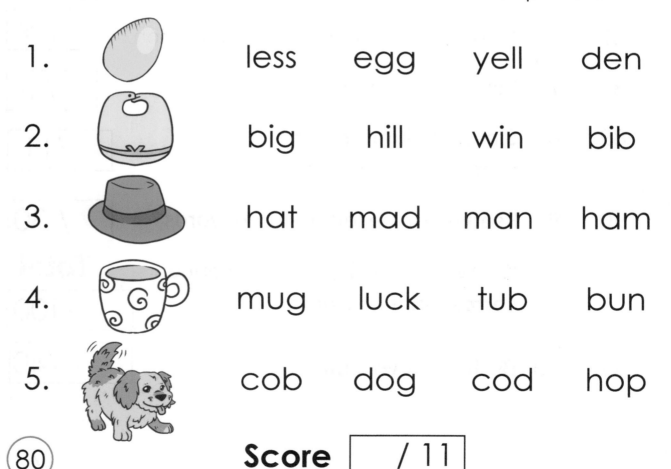

1. less   egg   yell   den

2. big   hill   win   bib

3. hat   mad   man   ham

4. mug   luck   tub   bun

5. cob   dog   cod   hop

Score   / 11

Test 3:2

Spelling; single letter-sound words

Say the rhyming words then write the missing word.

tap _____

well _____

wig _____

mop _____

Draw a line to match the words that rhyme

tax	pup	nod	neck
miss	yell	pat	rod
cup	wax	but	mat
sell	kiss	deck	nut

Score ___ / 12

Test 3:3

Spelling; single letter-sound words

Circle the correct letters and then write the word.

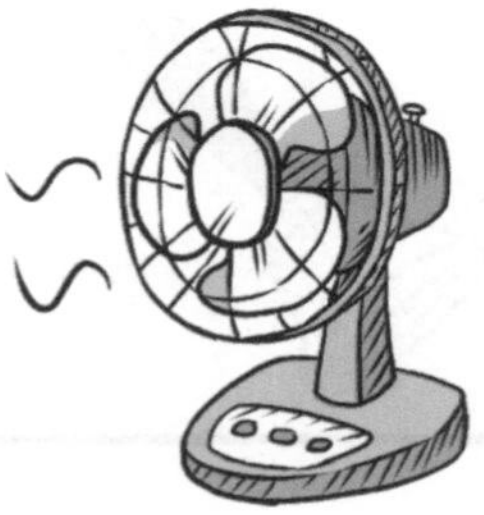	f c	i a	n t	
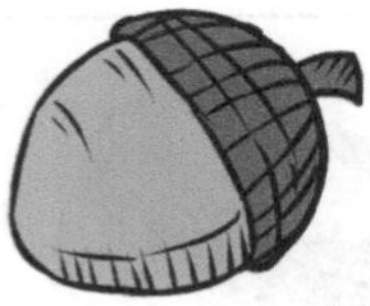	v n	o u	s t	
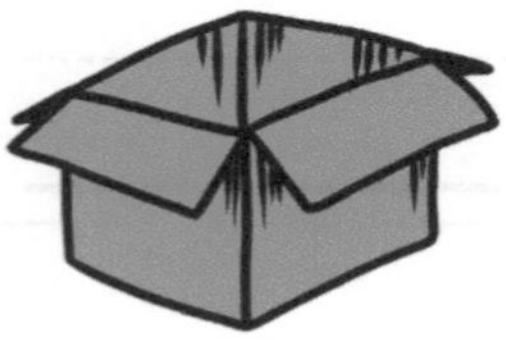	b r	e o	d x	
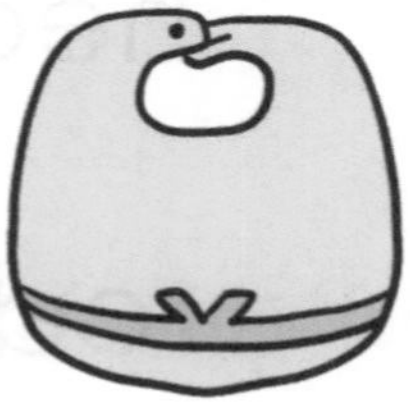	p b	i u	y b	
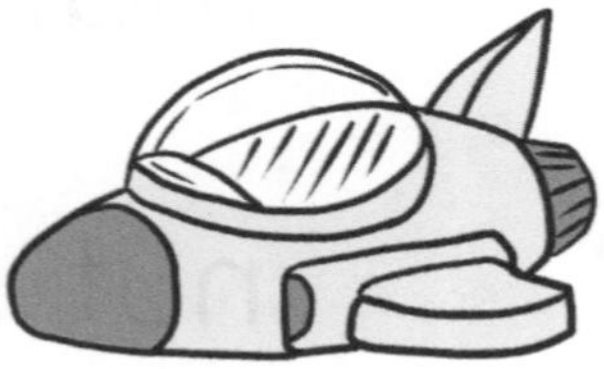	j h	a e	t k	

Score / 5

Test 3:4 | **Word recognition; word shape boxes**

Draw a line from the picture to the matching word.

sat
fat
bat

zip
lip
hip

not
pot
rot

gut
but
nut

Write the word that fits in the word shape box.

mix	loss	hug
rid	doll	bud
pig	lock	cup
kit	lot	bus

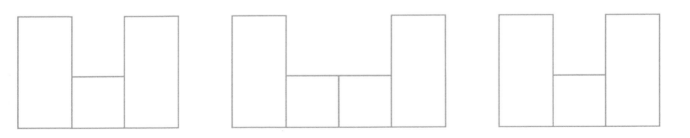

Score [/ 7]

Test 3:5

Write the words for the pictures.

1. _____

2. _____

3. _____

4. _____

5. _____

6. _____

7. _____

8. _____

9. _____

84

Score /9

Test 3:6

Crossword puzzles; word completion.

Write the words for the pictures in the spaces shown by arrows.

Write the missing letters in the spaces.

 1. P......m ......nd M......tt s......t in the v......n.

 2. P......g l......t the h......ns out of the p......n.

 3. D......d J......m p......ck up the b......n?

 4. The d......g h......ps ......n t......p of the r......ck.

 5. G......s h......ffs and p......ffs when he r......ns.

Score ☐ / 9

85

Test 3:7

Tick the sentence that describes the picture.

☐ Jan in her hat.

☐ Jan on the mat.

☐ The red pen is wet.

☐ The red hen is wet.

☐ My hog is in his log.

☐ My dog is in his log.

☐ The big pig has a wig.

☐ The big pig has a dig.

☐ Jill is on top of a pill.

☐ Jill is on top of a hill.

☐ I go for a run in the sun.

☐ I go for a run on a bun.

86

Score [/ 6]

Test 3:8   **Singular-plural spelling; sentence completion**

Write the word for the picture.

Write the word for the pictures.

1. Mum has a and six mugs.

2. Tom's dog sat on top of the .

3. The bug was in the .

4. Tess ran up the  .

5. The Tim got was too big.

Score ☐ / 11   87

Test 3:9

Single Letter-Sound Words

Read the words as quickly and accurately as possible.

fed	wag	hot
moss	gull	yell
sad	sock	win
buzz	hid	cut
dig	men	map
zip	fog	wax
rug	neck	fun
hat	cuff	sick
job	pit	yes
leg	tack	top

(88)

Score ⬚ / 30

Test 3:10

Basic sight vocabulary

Read these sight words as quickly and accurately as possible.

are	go	little	says
can	funny	of	play
boy	jump	look	run
come	is	my	red
and	he	like	said
to	big	in	it
this	away	here	not
see	down	good	me
at	for	have	man
the	blue	green	on

Score [/ 40]